Spotter's Guide to

GARD

FLOWERS

Barry Ambrose
of the Royal Horticultural Society's Garden, Wisley, England.

with additional material by Alexis Datta

Illustrated by William Giles

Contents

Editorial Director
Sue Jacquemier

Editors
Sue Tarsky, Rosamund Kidman Cox

Designer
William Giles

Additional illustrations by
Christine Howes

First published in 1978 by Usborne Publishing Limited, 20 Garrick Street, London WC2

Printed in Great Britain

The name Usborne and the device 🐝 are Trade Marks of Usborne Publishing Ltd.

Text and Artwork © 1978 by Usborne Publishing Limited

How to Use this Book

This book will help you to identify the most common garden flowers in Britain and Europe. Take it with you when you go out spotting.

The flowers are arranged by colour to make it easy for you to look them up. Remember that though the picture shows the flower as one colour, you may see the same flower in a different colour. For example, in the picture the Delphinium is blue, but it can also be mauve or white.

The pictures in circles next to the main illustrations show close-ups of flowers, or a plant's seeds or fruits. The fruits will help you to identify the plants in different seasons.

A description of each plant is given next to the picture. The plants are not drawn to scale, but their average heights from the ground to the tops of the flowers are given. The season in which the plant usually flowers in Britain is also given.

If a plant has a common name, that is the one used in the book. If it does not, the Latin name is used. Try and get someone who knows about gardening to say the Latin name aloud for you so you can learn to say it correctly.

Each time you spot a flower, make a tick in the small circle next to that flower's picture.

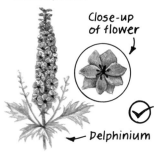

Close-up of flower

Delphinium

Scorecard

The scorecard at the end of the book gives you a score for each flower you spot. A flower which is easy to find scores 5 points and one which is uncommon, 25 points. Add up your scores after a day out spotting. You can tick off flowers if you see them in a different colour from the one illustrated in the book.

Page	Species (Name of Flower)	Score	Date May14	Date July1	Date July4
12	Cranesbill	15		15	15
13	Lilac	10	10		

What to Take

Take this book, a notebook and pencils with you, so that you can record your finds. Take a tape measure to measure the height of plants or the width of flowers. A magnifying glass will help you to have a closer look at the parts of flowers.

Draw flowers you spot and note down details about them. Be sure to include the height of the plant, the colour and shape of the flower head and the leaves, and where you found it

(for example, a rock garden or a greenhouse). If you find a flower that is not in this book, your drawing will help you to identify it from other books. There is a list of useful books on page 59.

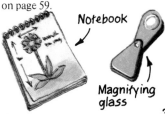

Notebook

Magnifying glass

What are Garden Flowers?

Rhododendron

Many garden flowers were originally wild plants. Some, like the Willow Gentian, were found wild in Britain and Europe. Others were found in tropical countries, e.g., the African Lily was first found in South Africa. Plant hunters went on special expeditions to find new and colourful plants that could be grown in gardens at home. The Rhododendron was first brought to Britain in 1656 after an expedition to the Alps.

Plant breeders then bred new forms of the plants, that were stronger, or were a different colour. If you go abroad on holiday, you may see garden plants growing wild. Because some garden plants, like the African Lily, come from hot countries, they like a lot of sun and grow best in a greenhouse.

Where to Find Garden Flowers

You do not need to have a garden to spot garden plants. You can find them in parks, zoos, in flower beds outside libraries, or school drives. Look in the windows of flower shops and garden shops. Look for window boxes and hanging baskets in towns, and flower tubs in shopping centres. In the country there are garden centres or nurseries, which sell plants. These are good places to go spotting, as most plants will have labels on them. Take your book if you visit a National Trust garden, or a stately home.

Useful Words

Hydrangea

◀ **Shrub:** woody stems and branches, but no single, central trunk like a tree. **Shrubby:** like a shrub. eg. Hydrangea.

Geranium

◀ **Bedding plant:** plant which can be grown in a greenhouse and then planted out in a flower bed. Usually small and short-lived, e.g. Geranium.

Evergreen: always green. Has leaves all the year.

Elephant's Ears

◀ **Ground cover:** plant which spreads well and covers a bare area of soil with its leaves.

Deciduous: drops all its leaves in winter. Opposite of evergreen.

Polyanthus

◀ **Perennial:** not woody like trees and shrubs. Lives for many years. Stores food in roots or underground stems.

4

Flowers and Flower Parts

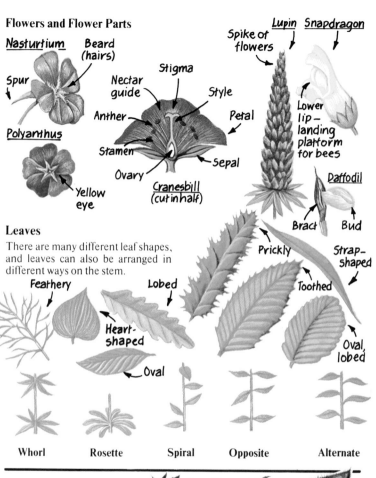

Nasturtium

Spur

Beard (hairs)

Polyanthus

Yellow eye

Nectar guide

Stigma

Style

Anther

Petal

Stamen

Ovary

Sepal

Cranesbill (cut in half)

Spike of flowers

Lupin **Snapdragon**

Lower lip – landing platform for bees

Daffodil

Bract   Bud

Leaves

There are many different leaf shapes, and leaves can also be arranged in different ways on the stem.

Feathery

Lobed

Prickly

Strap-shaped

Toothed

Heart-shaped

Oval

Oval, lobed

| Whorl | Rosette | Spiral | Opposite | Alternate |

Fruits and Seeds

Fruits are many sizes and shapes. They form after the flower petals have fallen off. Fruits may be juicy like the Rose hip, or dry like the Broom pod. Inside a fruit are the seeds. Seeds become new plants. Some gardeners collect their own seeds from plants.

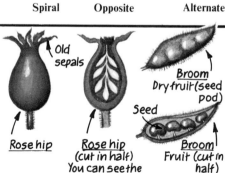

Old sepals

Rose hip

Rose hip (cut in half) You can see the seeds inside

Broom Dry fruit (seed pod)

Seed

Broom Fruit (cut in half)

5

Blue Flowers

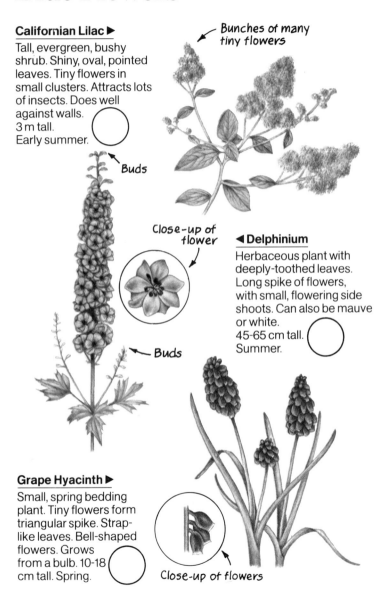

Californian Lilac ▶

Tall, evergreen, bushy shrub. Shiny, oval, pointed leaves. Tiny flowers in small clusters. Attracts lots of insects. Does well against walls.
3 m tall.
Early summer.

Bunches of many tiny flowers

Buds

Close-up of flower

◀ Delphinium

Herbaceous plant with deeply-toothed leaves. Long spike of flowers, with small, flowering side shoots. Can also be mauve or white.
45-65 cm tall.
Summer.

Buds

Grape Hyacinth ▶

Small, spring bedding plant. Tiny flowers form triangular spike. Strap-like leaves. Bell-shaped flowers. Grows from a bulb. 10-18 cm tall. Spring.

Close-up of flowers

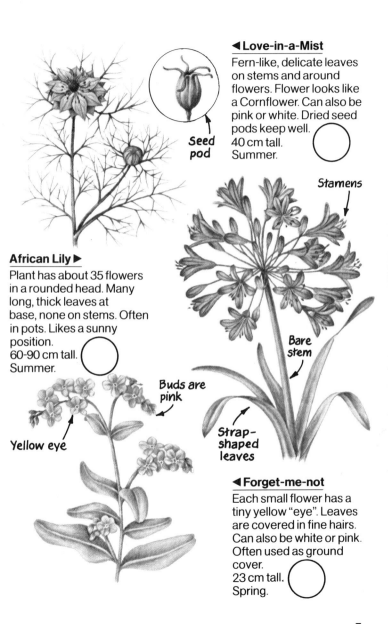

◄ Love-in-a-Mist

Fern-like, delicate leaves on stems and around flowers. Flower looks like a Cornflower. Can also be pink or white. Dried seed pods keep well.
40 cm tall.
Summer.

Seed pod

Stamens

African Lily ►

Plant has about 35 flowers in a rounded head. Many long, thick leaves at base, none on stems. Often in pots. Likes a sunny position.
60-90 cm tall.
Summer.

Bare stem

Buds are pink

Yellow eye

Strap-shaped leaves

◄ Forget-me-not

Each small flower has a tiny yellow "eye". Leaves are covered in fine hairs. Can also be white or pink. Often used as ground cover.
23 cm tall.
Spring.

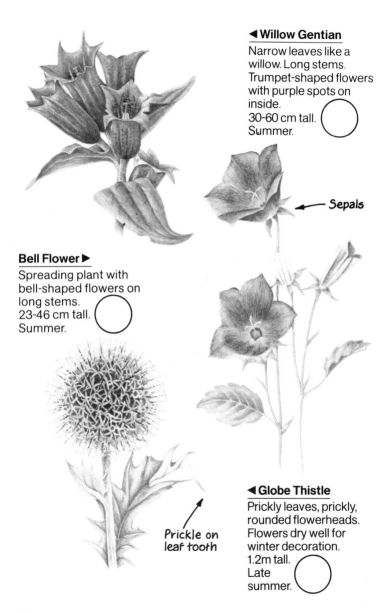

◄ Willow Gentian
Narrow leaves like a willow. Long stems. Trumpet-shaped flowers with purple spots on inside.
30-60 cm tall.
Summer.

Sepals

Bell Flower ►
Spreading plant with bell-shaped flowers on long stems.
23-46 cm tall.
Summer.

Prickle on leaf tooth

◄ Globe Thistle
Prickly leaves, prickly, rounded flowerheads. Flowers dry well for winter decoration.
1.2m tall.
Late summer.

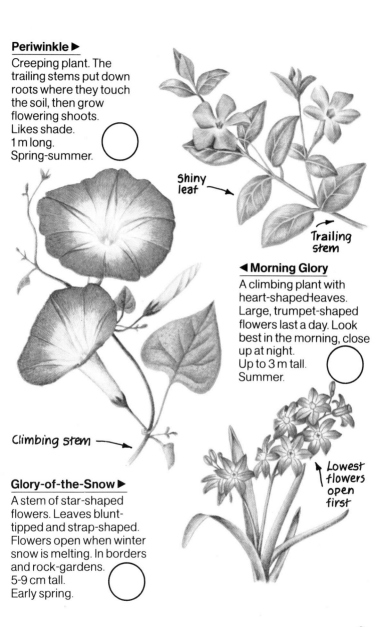

Periwinkle ▶
Creeping plant. The trailing stems put down roots where they touch the soil, then grow flowering shoots. Likes shade.
1 m long.
Spring-summer.

Shiny leaf →

→ Trailing stem

◀ Morning Glory
A climbing plant with heart-shaped leaves. Large, trumpet-shaped flowers last a day. Look best in the morning, close up at night.
Up to 3 m tall.
Summer.

Climbing stem —→

↓ Lowest flowers open first

Glory-of-the-Snow ▶
A stem of star-shaped flowers. Leaves blunt-tipped and strap-shaped. Flowers open when winter snow is melting. In borders and rock-gardens.
5-9 cm tall.
Early spring.

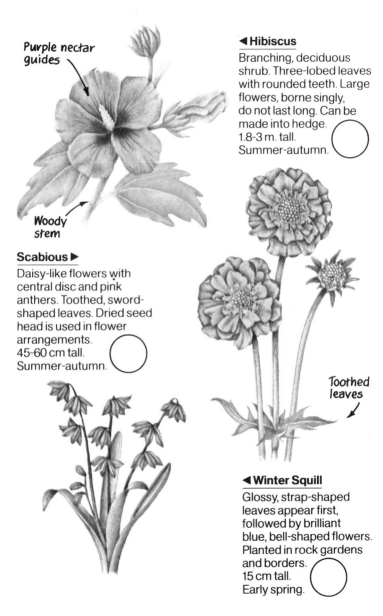

Purple nectar guides

Woody stem

◄ Hibiscus
Branching, deciduous shrub. Three-lobed leaves with rounded teeth. Large flowers, borne singly, do not last long. Can be made into hedge.
1.8-3 m. tall.
Summer-autumn.

Scabious ►
Daisy-like flowers with central disc and pink anthers. Toothed, sword-shaped leaves. Dried seed head is used in flower arrangements.
45-60 cm tall.
Summer-autumn.

Toothed leaves

◄ Winter Squill
Glossy, strap-shaped leaves appear first, followed by brilliant blue, bell-shaped flowers. Planted in rock gardens and borders.
15 cm tall.
Early spring.

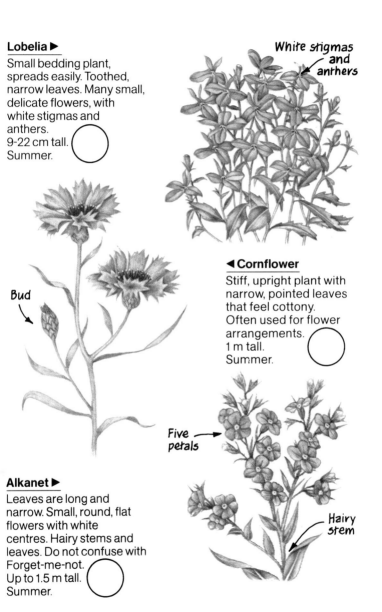

Lobelia ▶

Small bedding plant, spreads easily. Toothed, narrow leaves. Many small, delicate flowers, with white stigmas and anthers.
9-22 cm tall.
Summer.

White stigmas and anthers

Bud

◀ Cornflower

Stiff, upright plant with narrow, pointed leaves that feel cottony.
Often used for flower arrangements.
1 m tall.
Summer.

Five petals

Hairy stem

Alkanet ▶

Leaves are long and narrow. Small, round, flat flowers with white centres. Hairy stems and leaves. Do not confuse with Forget-me-not.
Up to 1.5 m tall.
Summer.

Purple Flowers

Aubretia deltoidea ▶

Look for this plant on walls, or in rock gardens. The flowers are small, and have four rounded petals. The leaves are hairy and toothed.
7-10 cm tall.
Spring.

Close-up of flower

◀ Wisteria

Hanging, scented, bunches of flowers. Oval, pointed leaves may appear after the flowers. Climbing shrub, often grown up walls. Up to 10 m high.
Spring-summer.

Woody main stem

Flowers may appear before leaves

Cranesbill ▶

Leaves deeply-lobed and toothed. Flowers deeper purple towards the centre, with long styles. Seed pod looks like a bird's head and beak.
30-60 cm tall.
Mid-summer.

Young seed pod

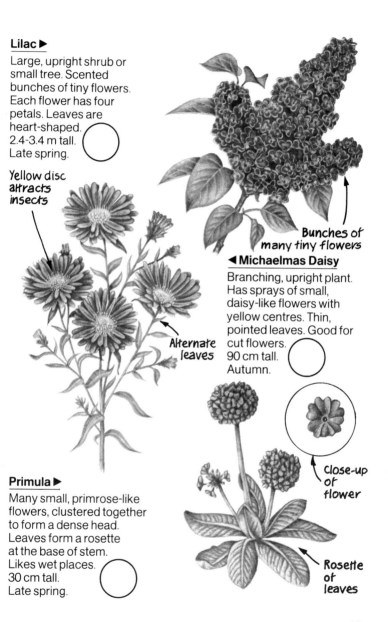

Lilac ▶

Large, upright shrub or small tree. Scented bunches of tiny flowers. Each flower has four petals. Leaves are heart-shaped. 2.4-3.4 m tall. Late spring.

Yellow disc attracts insects

Bunches of many tiny flowers

◀ Michaelmas Daisy

Branching, upright plant. Has sprays of small, daisy-like flowers with yellow centres. Thin, pointed leaves. Good for cut flowers. 90 cm tall. Autumn.

Alternate leaves

Close-up of flower

Primula ▶

Many small, primrose-like flowers, clustered together to form a dense head. Leaves form a rosette at the base of stem. Likes wet places. 30 cm tall. Late spring.

Rosette of leaves

13

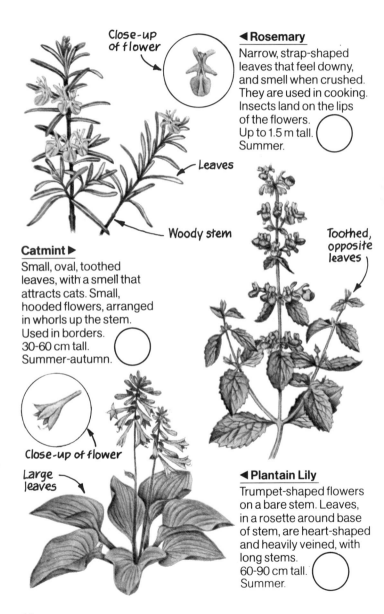

Close-up of flower

◄ Rosemary
Narrow, strap-shaped leaves that feel downy, and smell when crushed. They are used in cooking. Insects land on the lips of the flowers. Up to 1.5 m tall. Summer.

Leaves

Woody stem

Toothed, opposite leaves

Catmint ►
Small, oval, toothed leaves, with a smell that attracts cats. Small, hooded flowers, arranged in whorls up the stem. Used in borders. 30-60 cm tall. Summer-autumn.

Close-up of flower

Large leaves

◄ Plantain Lily
Trumpet-shaped flowers on a bare stem. Leaves, in a rosette around base of stem, are heart-shaped and heavily veined, with long stems. 60-90 cm tall. Summer.

Hebe ▶

Evergreen, flowering shrub.
Small, tight, bunches of
tiny flowers, with four
different-sized petals.
Long style and stamens.
Glossy leaves.
Up to 1.2 m tall.
Summer-autumn.

Long stamens and styles

Flower head is made up of tiny flowers

Shiny leaves

◀ Buddleia or Butterfly Bush

Tall, shrubby plant which
attracts butterflies.
Long, upright, bunches of
tiny flowers with sweet
scent. Long, pointed
leaves.
2.7 m tall.
Summer-autumn.

Flower spike

Lavender ▶

Spike of flowers at
end of long, square
stem. Stem and leaves are
downy. Long, thin leaves.
Dried flowers are used in
lavender bags.
Up to 1.2 m tall.
Summer.

Leaves smell when rubbed

15

Pink Flowers

Very young leaves

◀ Pink Magnolia
Large, woody shrub. Goblet-shaped flowers have petals that drop off easily. They bloom on bare branches. Leaves appear later.
3-5 m tall.
Spring.

Petals drop off easily

Rose Campion ▶
Flowers bloom for short time only. May also be white. Branching stems. Opposite leaves are soft, woolly, whitish and pointed.
Up to 60 cm tall.
Mid–late summer.

Opposite leaves

Glossy leaves

Pink flower stalk

◀ Elephant's Ears
Large clusters of small, bell-shaped flowers on a pink flower stem. Large, oval, glossy leaves. Likes shade. Used as ground cover.
30 cm tall.
Spring.

Weigela ▶
Wide-spreading bush with arched branches. Trumpet-shaped flowers grow in clusters, bloom for a short time. Oval, toothed leaves.
1.8 m tall.
Early summer.

Five petals joined into tube

Five petals

◀ Pink
Fragrant, flat flowers. Fringed petals. Long-lived. Greyish-white stem and leaves. Leaves are thin and pointed. Used in rock gardens.
12-30 cm tall.
Summer.

Style longer than stamens

Rhododendron ▶
Large, evergreen shrub. Flower heads made up of funnel-shaped flowers, each 6-8 cm across. Large, oval leaves. Can be other colours.
3-4.5 m tall.
Spring-summer.

Glossy leaves

17

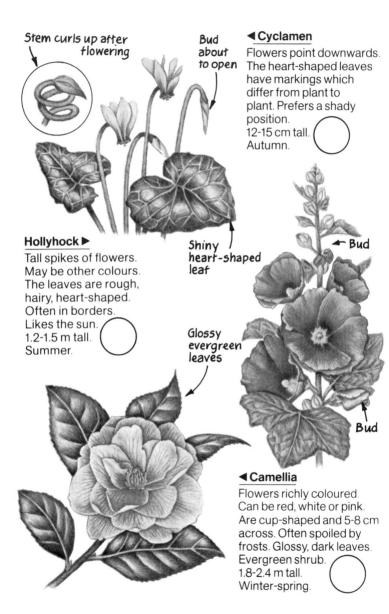

Stem curls up after flowering

Bud about to open

◀ Cyclamen

Flowers point downwards. The heart-shaped leaves have markings which differ from plant to plant. Prefers a shady position.
12-15 cm tall.
Autumn.

Hollyhock ▶

Tall spikes of flowers. May be other colours. The leaves are rough, hairy, heart-shaped. Often in borders. Likes the sun.
1.2-1.5 m tall.
Summer.

Shiny heart-shaped leaf

Bud

Glossy evergreen leaves

Bud

◀ Camellia

Flowers richly coloured. Can be red, white or pink. Are cup-shaped and 5-8 cm across. Often spoiled by frosts. Glossy, dark leaves. Evergreen shrub.
1.8-2.4 m tall.
Winter-spring.

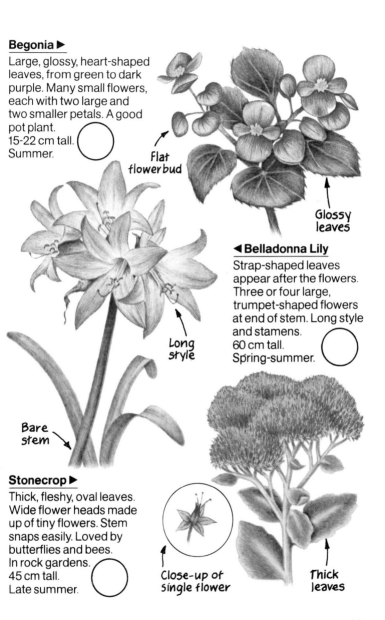

Begonia ▶

Large, glossy, heart-shaped leaves, from green to dark purple. Many small flowers, each with two large and two smaller petals. A good pot plant.
15-22 cm tall.
Summer.

Flat flower bud

Glossy leaves

◀ Belladonna Lily

Strap-shaped leaves appear after the flowers. Three or four large, trumpet-shaped flowers at end of stem. Long style and stamens.
60 cm tall.
Spring-summer.

Long style

Bare stem

Stonecrop ▶

Thick, fleshy, oval leaves. Wide flower heads made up of tiny flowers. Stem snaps easily. Loved by butterflies and bees. In rock gardens.
45 cm tall.
Late summer.

Close-up of single flower

Thick leaves

Red Flowers

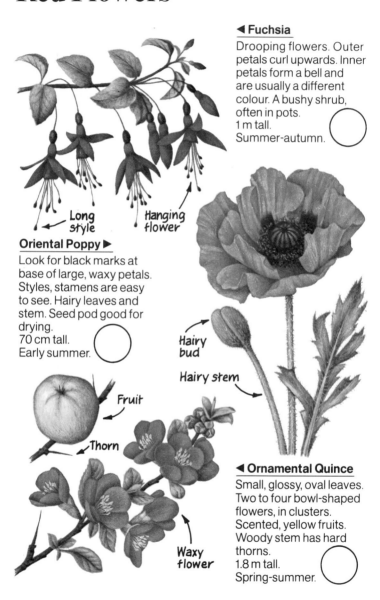

◄ Fuchsia

Drooping flowers. Outer petals curl upwards. Inner petals form a bell and are usually a different colour. A bushy shrub, often in pots.
1 m tall.
Summer-autumn.

Long style

Hanging flower

Oriental Poppy ►

Look for black marks at base of large, waxy petals. Styles, stamens are easy to see. Hairy leaves and stem. Seed pod good for drying.
70 cm tall.
Early summer.

Hairy bud

Hairy stem

Fruit

Thorn

◄ Ornamental Quince

Small, glossy, oval leaves. Two to four bowl-shaped flowers, in clusters. Scented, yellow fruits. Woody stem has hard thorns.
1.8 m tall.
Spring-summer.

Waxy flower

20

Escallonia macrantha ▶

Clusters of flowers with red flower stems. Small, oval, toothed, glossy leaves. Can stand salt spray and sea gales. Hedging plant. 1.8 m tall. Summer-autumn.

Flowers have red stems

Red bracts

Circle of flowers around stem

◀ Oswego Tea

Bright red flowers attract bees and butterflies. Scented leaves can be dried and used in tea. Whorls of red bracts below whorls of flowers. 60-90 cm tall. Summer.

Red fruit called a "hip"

Flat flower

Rosa moyesii ▶

A tall shrub rose. Red flowers are followed by shiny red fruits that look like small bottles. Stem usually thinner than in Tea Roses. Up to 2 m tall. Mid-summer.

21

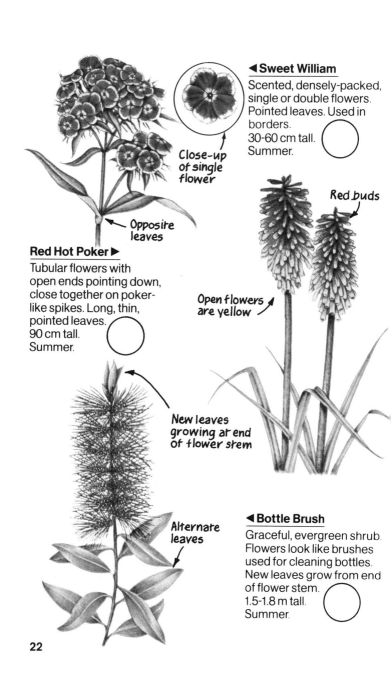

◄ Sweet William
Scented, densely-packed, single or double flowers. Pointed leaves. Used in borders.
30-60 cm tall.
Summer.

Close-up of single flower

Opposite leaves

Red buds

Red Hot Poker ▶
Tubular flowers with open ends pointing down, close together on poker-like spikes. Long, thin, pointed leaves.
90 cm tall.
Summer.

Open flowers are yellow

New leaves growing at end of flower stem

Alternate leaves

◄ Bottle Brush
Graceful, evergreen shrub. Flowers look like brushes used for cleaning bottles. New leaves grow from end of flower stem.
1.5-1.8 m tall.
Summer.

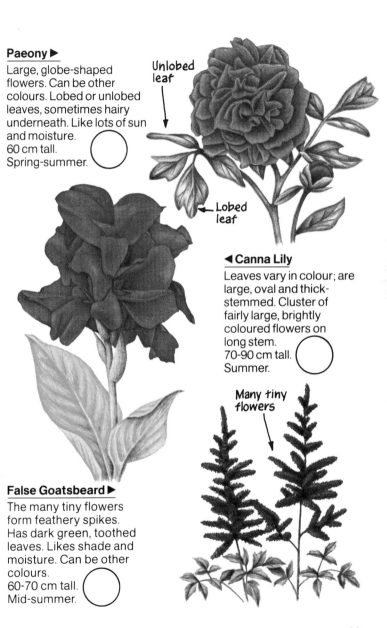

Paeony ▶

Large, globe-shaped flowers. Can be other colours. Lobed or unlobed leaves, sometimes hairy underneath. Like lots of sun and moisture.
60 cm tall.
Spring-summer.

Unlobed leaf

Lobed leaf

◀ Canna Lily

Leaves vary in colour; are large, oval and thick-stemmed. Cluster of fairly large, brightly coloured flowers on long stem.
70-90 cm tall.
Summer.

Many tiny flowers

False Goatsbeard ▶

The many tiny flowers form feathery spikes. Has dark green, toothed leaves. Likes shade and moisture. Can be other colours.
60-70 cm tall.
Mid-summer.

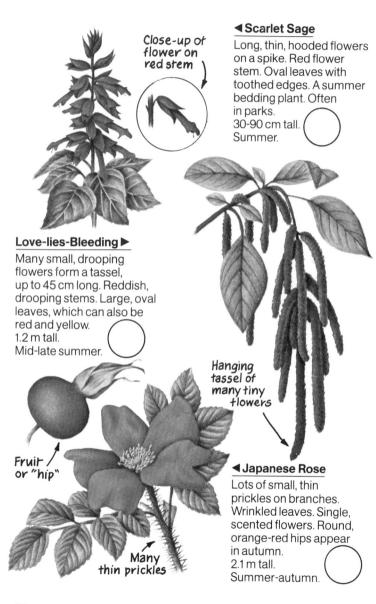

Close-up of flower on red stem

◀ Scarlet Sage

Long, thin, hooded flowers on a spike. Red flower stem. Oval leaves with toothed edges. A summer bedding plant. Often in parks.
30-90 cm tall.
Summer.

Love-lies-Bleeding ▶

Many small, drooping flowers form a tassel, up to 45 cm long. Reddish, drooping stems. Large, oval leaves, which can also be red and yellow.
1.2 m tall.
Mid-late summer.

Hanging tassel of many tiny flowers

Fruit or "hip"

◀ Japanese Rose

Lots of small, thin prickles on branches. Wrinkled leaves. Single, scented flowers. Round, orange-red hips appear in autumn.
2.1 m tall.
Summer-autumn.

Many thin prickles

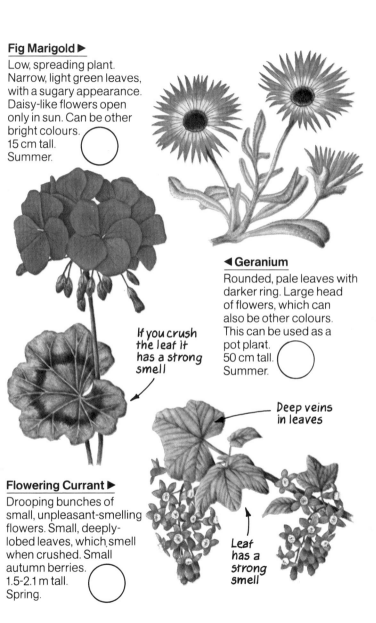

Fig Marigold ▶
Low, spreading plant.
Narrow, light green leaves,
with a sugary appearance.
Daisy-like flowers open
only in sun. Can be other
bright colours.
15 cm tall.
Summer.

◀ Geranium
Rounded, pale leaves with
darker ring. Large head
of flowers, which can
also be other colours.
This can be used as a
pot plant.
50 cm tall.
Summer.

If you crush
the leaf it
has a strong
smell

Deep veins
in leaves

Flowering Currant ▶
Drooping bunches of
small, unpleasant-smelling
flowers. Small, deeply-
lobed leaves, which smell
when crushed. Small
autumn berries.
1.5-2.1 m tall.
Spring.

Leaf
has a
strong
smell

Orange Flowers

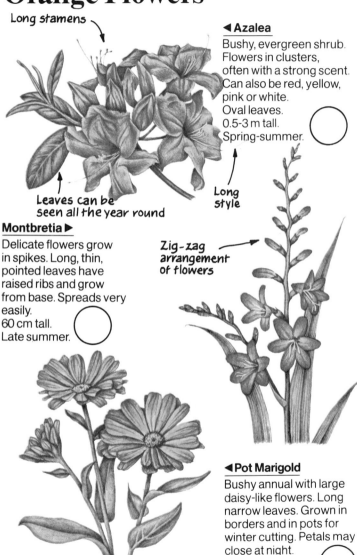

Long stamens

◀ Azalea
Bushy, evergreen shrub.
Flowers in clusters,
often with a strong scent.
Can also be red, yellow,
pink or white.
Oval leaves.
0.5-3 m tall.
Spring-summer.

Leaves can be
seen all the year round

Long
style

Montbretia ▶
Delicate flowers grow
in spikes. Long, thin,
pointed leaves have
raised ribs and grow
from base. Spreads very
easily.
60 cm tall.
Late summer.

Zig-zag
arrangement
of flowers

◀ Pot Marigold
Bushy annual with large
daisy-like flowers. Long
narrow leaves. Grown in
borders and in pots for
winter cutting. Petals may
close at night.
30-40 cm tall.
Summer-autumn.

◄ Day Lily

Herbaceous plants,
forming large clumps.
Flowers have long
style and stamens; last
one day. Arching, strap-like
leaves.
0.6-1.0 m tall.
Mid-summer.

Crown Imperial ►

Narrow, glossy leaves.
Bell-shaped flowers hang
in clusters under leaves.
Have long stamens
hanging below petals.
Brown stem.
60-90 cm tall.
Spring.

Flowers
under
leaves

Long
stamens

Spur

◄ Nasturtium

Faintly scented, trumpet-
shaped flowers. Leaves
have wavy edges and
smell like cabbages.
Climbing or trailing
plants.
20-40 cm tall.
Summer-autumn.

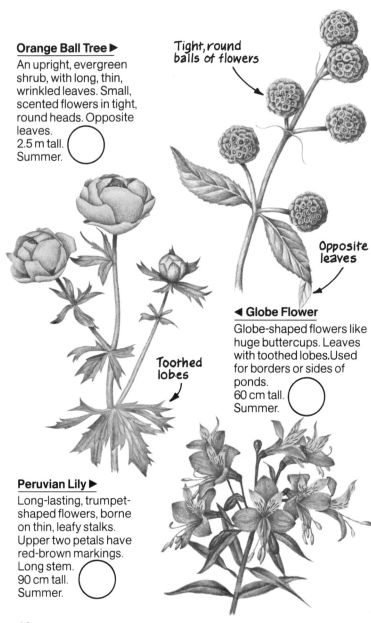

Orange Ball Tree ▶

An upright, evergreen shrub, with long, thin, wrinkled leaves. Small, scented flowers in tight, round heads. Opposite leaves.
2.5 m tall.
Summer.

Tight, round balls of flowers

Opposite leaves

Toothed lobes

◀ Globe Flower

Globe-shaped flowers like huge buttercups. Leaves with toothed lobes.Used for borders or sides of ponds.
60 cm tall.
Summer.

Peruvian Lily ▶

Long-lasting, trumpet-shaped flowers, borne on thin, leafy stalks. Upper two petals have red-brown markings.
Long stem.
90 cm tall.
Summer.

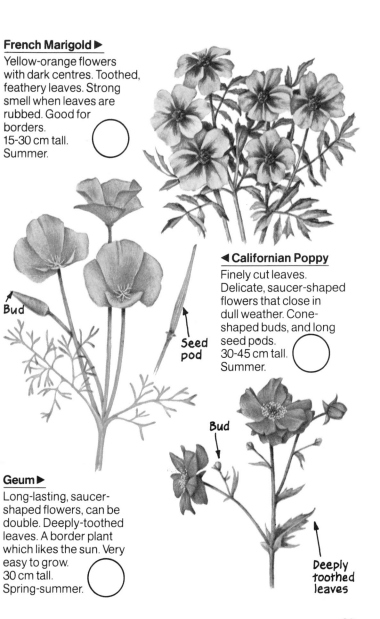

French Marigold ▶

Yellow-orange flowers with dark centres. Toothed, feathery leaves. Strong smell when leaves are rubbed. Good for borders.
15-30 cm tall.
Summer.

Bud

Seed pod

◀ Californian Poppy

Finely cut leaves. Delicate, saucer-shaped flowers that close in dull weather. Cone-shaped buds, and long seed pods.
30-45 cm tall.
Summer.

Bud

Geum ▶

Long-lasting, saucer-shaped flowers, can be double. Deeply-toothed leaves. A border plant which likes the sun. Very easy to grow.
30 cm tall.
Spring-summer.

Deeply toothed leaves

White Flowers

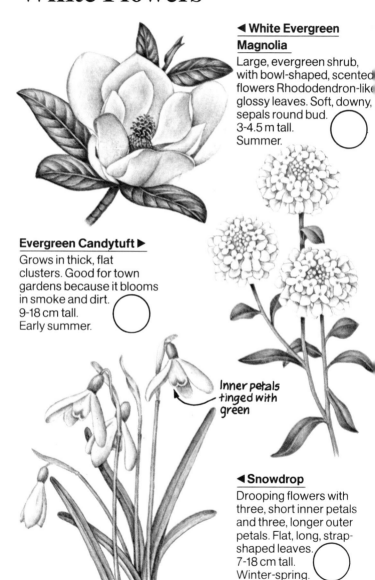

◄ White Evergreen Magnolia

Large, evergreen shrub, with bowl-shaped, scented flowers Rhododendron-like glossy leaves. Soft, downy, sepals round bud.
3-4.5 m tall.
Summer.

Evergreen Candytuft ►

Grows in thick, flat clusters. Good for town gardens because it blooms in smoke and dirt.
9-18 cm tall.
Early summer.

Inner petals tinged with green

◄ Snowdrop

Drooping flowers with three, short inner petals and three, longer outer petals. Flat, long, strap-shaped leaves.
7-18 cm tall.
Winter-spring.

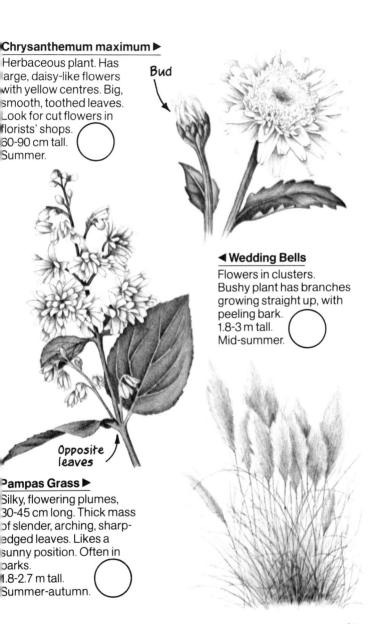

Chrysanthemum maximum ▶

Herbaceous plant. Has
large, daisy-like flowers
with yellow centres. Big,
smooth, toothed leaves.
Look for cut flowers in
florists' shops.
60-90 cm tall.
Summer.

Bud

◀ Wedding Bells

Flowers in clusters.
Bushy plant has branches
growing straight up, with
peeling bark.
1.8-3 m tall.
Mid-summer.

Opposite
leaves

Pampas Grass ▶

Silky, flowering plumes,
30-45 cm long. Thick mass
of slender, arching, sharp-
edged leaves. Likes a
sunny position. Often in
parks.
1.8-2.7 m tall.
Summer-autumn.

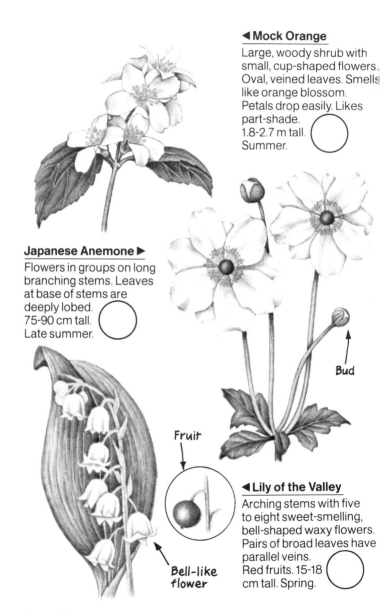

◀ Mock Orange

Large, woody shrub with small, cup-shaped flowers. Oval, veined leaves. Smells like orange blossom. Petals drop easily. Likes part-shade. 1.8-2.7 m tall. Summer.

Japanese Anemone ▶

Flowers in groups on long branching stems. Leaves at base of stems are deeply lobed. 75-90 cm tall. Late summer.

Bud

Fruit

◀ Lily of the Valley

Arching stems with five to eight sweet-smelling, bell-shaped waxy flowers. Pairs of broad leaves have parallel veins. Red fruits. 15-18 cm tall. Spring.

Bell-like flower

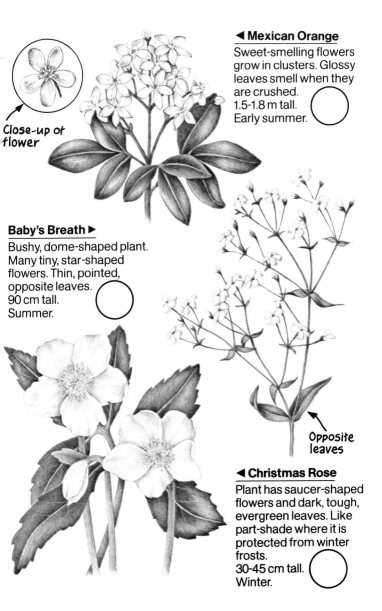

Close-up of flower

◄ Mexican Orange

Sweet-smelling flowers grow in clusters. Glossy leaves smell when they are crushed.
1.5-1.8 m tall.
Early summer.

Baby's Breath ►

Bushy, dome-shaped plant. Many tiny, star-shaped flowers. Thin, pointed, opposite leaves.
90 cm tall.
Summer.

Opposite leaves

◄ Christmas Rose

Plant has saucer-shaped flowers and dark, tough, evergreen leaves. Like part-shade where it is protected from winter frosts.
30-45 cm tall.
Winter.

Rock Cress

Small, evergreen plant,
grown on walls and banks.
Long, rounded leaves.
Small, flowers with four
petals. Sweetly scented.
Easy to grow.
20 cm tall.
Spring-summer.

Pink buds

Glossy
leaves

◀ Viburnum tinus

Bushy evergreen shrub
with pointed oval leaves.
Small flowers are in a
flat head, 6-8 cm across.
Sweet smell.
2-3 m tall.
Winter-spring.

Orange
anthers

Yellow
stigma

Madonna Lily ▶

Tall upright plant with
long, strap-shaped leaves.
Hanging flowers, 7-9 cm
long, born singly on the
stem. Bright orange
anthers. Sweet
scented. 1.5 m
tall. Summer.

Yellow Flowers

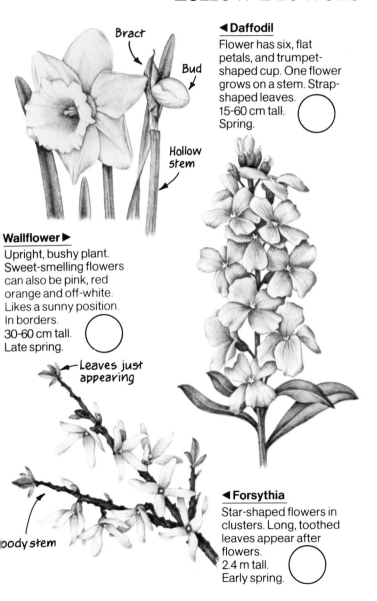

Bract

Bud

Hollow stem

◄ Daffodil
Flower has six, flat petals, and trumpet-shaped cup. One flower grows on a stem. Strap-shaped leaves.
15-60 cm tall.
Spring.

Wallflower ►
Upright, bushy plant. Sweet-smelling flowers can also be pink, red orange and off-white. Likes a sunny position. In borders.
30-60 cm tall.
Late spring.

Leaves just appearing

Woody stem

◄ Forsythia
Star-shaped flowers in clusters. Long, toothed leaves appear after flowers.
2.4 m tall.
Early spring.

35

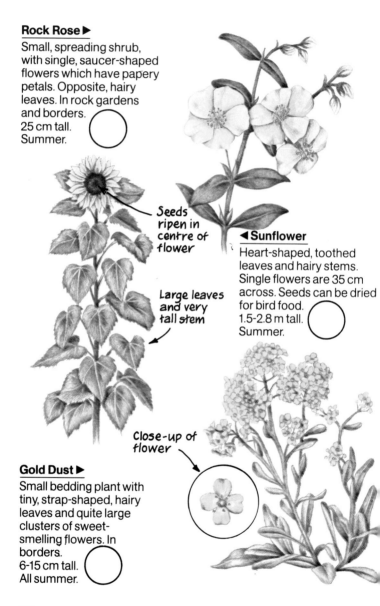

Rock Rose ▶

Small, spreading shrub, with single, saucer-shaped flowers which have papery petals. Opposite, hairy leaves. In rock gardens and borders.
25 cm tall.
Summer.

Seeds ripen in centre of flower

Large leaves and very tall stem

◀ Sunflower

Heart-shaped, toothed leaves and hairy stems. Single flowers are 35 cm across. Seeds can be dried for bird food.
1.5-2.8 m tall.
Summer.

Close-up of flower

Gold Dust ▶

Small bedding plant with tiny, strap-shaped, hairy leaves and quite large clusters of sweet-smelling flowers. In borders.
6-15 cm tall.
All summer.

Winter Aconite ▶

One cup-shaped flower on a stem, with a circle of deeply cut, pale leaves under it. Seeds spread easily. In borders and under trees.
10 cm tall.
Early spring.

Whorl of leaves around flower

Bare stems

Masses of tiny flowers

◀ Golden Rod

Tiny, feathery flowers form clusters. Long leaves, rough on top, at alternate points up stem. In sunny borders.
Up to 1.8 m tall.
Summer-autumn.

Senecio 'Sunshine' ▶

Daisy-like flowers grow in clusters. Thick, oval-shaped leaves have greyish-white felt on undersides. Can be quite bushy.
Up to 1.2 m tall.
Summer.

White underside of leaf

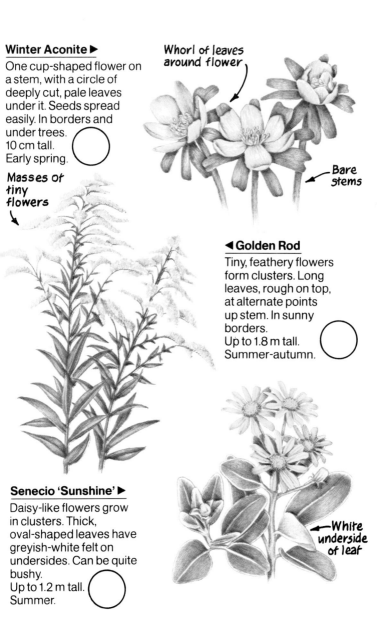

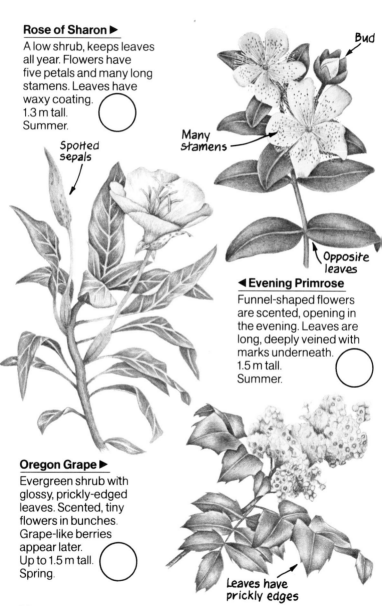

Rose of Sharon ▶

A low shrub, keeps leaves all year. Flowers have five petals and many long stamens. Leaves have waxy coating.
1.3 m tall.
Summer.

Bud

Many stamens

Spotted sepals

Opposite leaves

◀ Evening Primrose

Funnel-shaped flowers are scented, opening in the evening. Leaves are long, deeply veined with marks underneath.
1.5 m tall.
Summer.

Oregon Grape ▶

Evergreen shrub with glossy, prickly-edged leaves. Scented, tiny flowers in bunches. Grape-like berries appear later.
Up to 1.5 m tall.
Spring.

Leaves have prickly edges

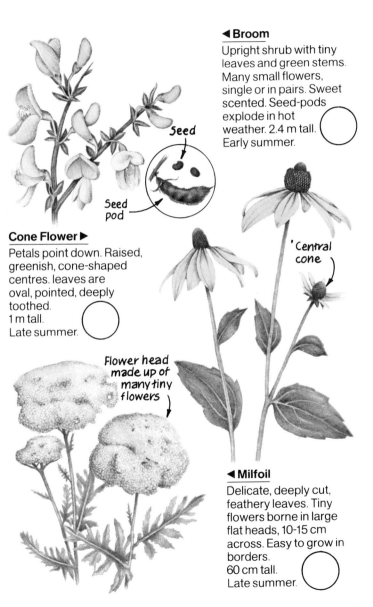

◀ Broom
Upright shrub with tiny leaves and green stems. Many small flowers, single or in pairs. Sweet scented. Seed-pods explode in hot weather. 2.4 m tall. Early summer.

Seed

Seed pod

Cone Flower ▶
Petals point down. Raised, greenish, cone-shaped centres. leaves are oval, pointed, deeply toothed.
1 m tall.
Late summer.

'Central cone

Flower head made up of many tiny flowers

◀ Milfoil
Delicate, deeply cut, feathery leaves. Tiny flowers borne in large flat heads, 10-15 cm across. Easy to grow in borders.
60 cm tall.
Late summer.

Potentilla fructicosa ▶

Look in borders and rock gardens. Saucer-shaped flowers have five petals. A shrub, with tough stems and many branches. Likes a sunny position.
1.2-1.5 m tall.
Spring-autumn.

Five petals

Bud

◀ Leopard's Bane

Daisy-like flowers on long stalks. Toothed, heart-shaped leaves. In borders, but prefers semi-shade. Good for cut flowers.
60 cm tall.
Spring-summer.

Bud

Honeysuckle ▶

Long, tube-shaped, scented flowers growing in clusters. Only lower leaves are on stalks. Poisonous fruit in autumn. A climber.
2-3 m tall.
Summer.

Stalkless leaves

Stalked leaves

Cluster of fruit

Winter Jasmine ▶

Flowers appear before the leaves. Small, trumpet-shaped flowers. Tough, deep green stem. Small glossy leaves. Can be trained to grow up walls. Up to 3 m tall. Winter.

Deep green stem

◀ Sneezeweed

Long, thin, toothed leaves. Flowers with wavy-edged petals and large central discs. Look in sunny borders. Makes good cut flowers. 90 cm tall. Summer-autumn.

Tickweed ▶

The petals have ragged edges. Long thin leaves and round buds. Spreads easily and makes good cut flowers. Look in borders. 30-45 cm tall. Summer.

Flowers that can be Various Colours

Close-up of flower

Yellow eye

◀ Polyanthus
Clusters of primrose-like flowers on stout stems, with rosette of leaves at base. Can be a variety of colours. Suitable for window-boxes.
15 cm tall.
Summer.

Lupin ▶
A spike of small flowers, 60 cm tall. Leaf made up of 5-15 small leaves. Spreads easily. Found in borders.
Up to 1.5 m tall.
Summer.

Spike of flowers

◀ China Aster
Large, round flower, with lots of petals. Hairy, deeply-lobed leaves. Look in sunny borders. Good cut flowers.
20-30 cm tall.
Summer.

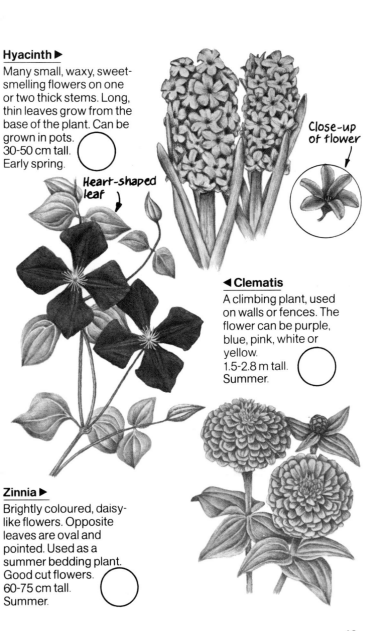

Hyacinth ▶

Many small, waxy, sweet-smelling flowers on one or two thick stems. Long, thin leaves grow from the base of the plant. Can be grown in pots.
30-50 cm tall.
Early spring.

Close-up of flower

Heart-shaped leaf

◀ Clematis

A climbing plant, used on walls or fences. The flower can be purple, blue, pink, white or yellow.
1.5-2.8 m tall.
Summer.

Zinnia ▶

Brightly coloured, daisy-like flowers. Opposite leaves are oval and pointed. Used as a summer bedding plant. Good cut flowers.
60-75 cm tall.
Summer.

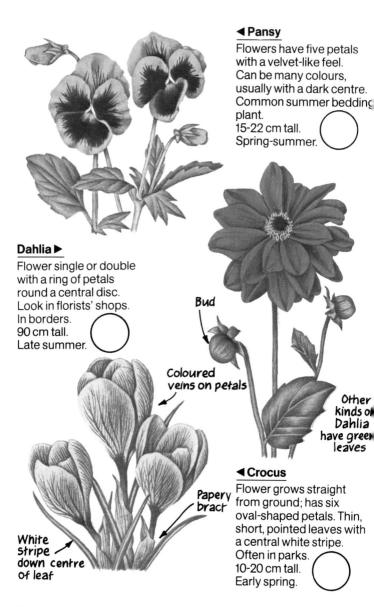

◀ Pansy

Flowers have five petals with a velvet-like feel. Can be many colours, usually with a dark centre. Common summer bedding plant.
15-22 cm tall.
Spring-summer.

Dahlia ▶

Flower single or double with a ring of petals round a central disc. Look in florists' shops. In borders.
90 cm tall.
Late summer.

Bud

Coloured veins on petals

Other kinds of Dahlia have green leaves

Papery bract

White stripe down centre of leaf

◀ Crocus

Flower grows straight from ground; has six oval-shaped petals. Thin, short, pointed leaves with a central white stripe. Often in parks.
10-20 cm tall.
Early spring.

Hybrid Tea Rose ▶

The familiar Rose.
Sweet-smelling flowers
with cone-shaped buds.
Prickly stems and glossy
leaves in groups. Amber
hips in autumn.
Up to 1.2 m tall.
All summer.

Close-up
of flower

Petals are
joined to
form a
tube

◀ Foxglove

Spotted, bell-shaped
flowers grow on one
side only of tall spike.
Leaves grow from base
of spike.
Up to 1.5 m tall.
Summer-autumn.

Phlox ▶

Sweet-smelling, flat
flowers grow in clusters.
Long, thin leaves. Often
used in borders. Good for
cut flowers.
Up to 1.2 m tall.
Summer-autumn.

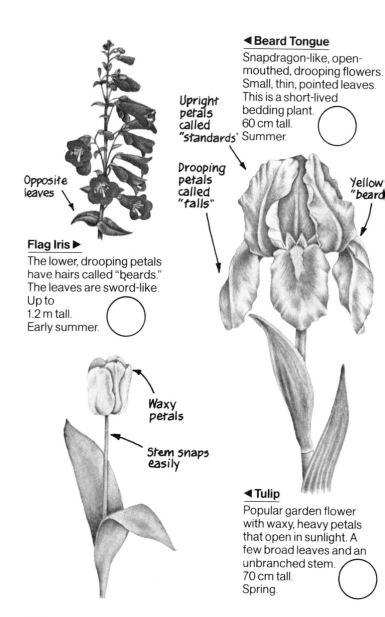

Opposite
leaves

Flag Iris ▶
The lower, drooping petals
have hairs called "beards."
The leaves are sword-like.
Up to
1.2 m tall.
Early summer.

Upright
petals
called
"standards"

Drooping
petals
called
"falls"

◀ Beard Tongue
Snapdragon-like, open-
mouthed, drooping flowers.
Small, thin, pointed leaves.
This is a short-lived
bedding plant.
60 cm tall.
Summer.

Yellow
"beard"

Waxy
petals

Stem snaps
easily

◀ Tulip
Popular garden flower
with waxy, heavy petals
that open in sunlight. A
few broad leaves and an
unbranched stem.
70 cm tall.
Spring.

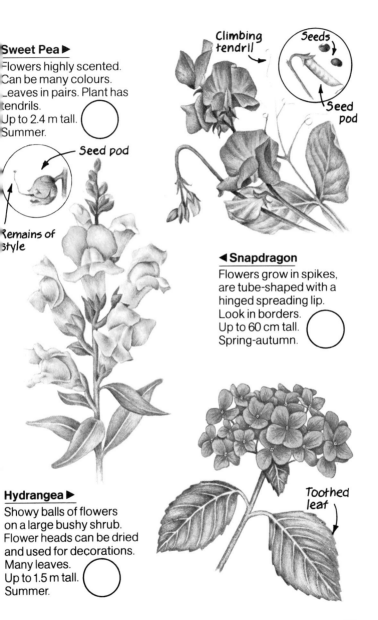

Sweet Pea ▶
Flowers highly scented.
Can be many colours.
Leaves in pairs. Plant has
tendrils.
Up to 2.4 m tall.
Summer.

Seed pod

Remains of
style

Climbing
tendril

Seeds

Seed
pod

◀ Snapdragon
Flowers grow in spikes,
are tube-shaped with a
hinged spreading lip.
Look in borders.
Up to 60 cm tall.
Spring-autumn.

Toothed
leaf

Hydrangea ▶
Showy balls of flowers
on a large bushy shrub.
Flower heads can be dried
and used for decorations.
Many leaves.
Up to 1.5 m tall.
Summer.

Petunia ▶

Look in flower beds. A low-growing plant with large, trumpet-shaped, open flowers. Leaves are pointed and oval. Used in window boxes.
30-45 cm tall.
Summer.

Bud

◀ Gladiolus

The flowers all face the same way on thick stems, and grow to form a spike. Sword-shaped leaves. In borders. Also look in florists' shops.
45-85 cm tall.
Mid-summer.

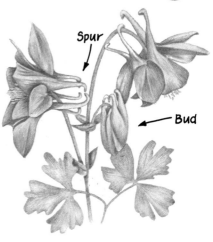

Spur

Bud

Columbine ▶

Nodding, delicate flowers. Look for long, showy spurs on petals. Branching stems with a single flower on each one.
Up to 1 m tall.
Late spring.

Easy Gardening

The most important tools you need are a spade, fork, rake and a trowel. A hoe, hand fork and hand hoe are also useful. Ask an adult if you can borrow these tools, but be sure to clean them each time you have finished with them. Never leave any equipment lying on the ground – it is easy to trip over a handle or step on a rake by accident. Wear thick-soled shoes to protect your feet.

Find out what conditions your plants like best (the kind of soil, amount of water, amount of sun) so that you can help them to grow well. Read the directions on seed packets before you plant. When you know the height, shape and colour a plant will be, you can decide where to put it, and how far away from other plants it should be.

Most plants like sun, but some need less than others. Choose flowers that need sun only part of the day for the shadier places in your garden, and plant the rest in sunny spots. Remember that some plants need more water than others.

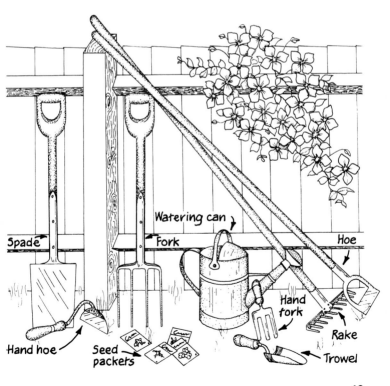

Spade

Fork

Watering can

Hoe

Hand fork

Hand hoe

Seed packets

Rake

Trowel

Growing Annuals

The plants shown below are annuals. These are plants that only live for one season. The seed packets will tell you which plants are annuals. If you sow the seed in spring, the plant will flower in summer and then die before the winter

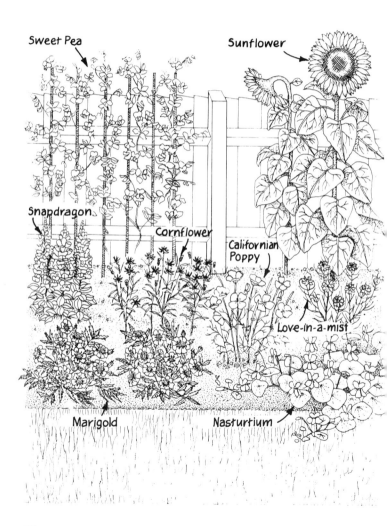

Choose an unshaded bit of ground and dig it over in winter, so that the rain and frost help break up the soil. In spring, pull up weeds and take out stones. Rake the soil level.

With a stick, make even lines (called drills) in the soil, in which to sow the seeds. Make the drills far enough apart so that the plants have room to grow. Sow the seeds thinly.

The seed packets will tell you when to sow the seeds and how far down in the ground to plant them. Carefully rake soil back over the seeds and gently pat it down.

Write the names of the plants and dates of sowing on lollipop sticks, or on labels and push them in at the end of the drills so you know where you have sown which seeds.

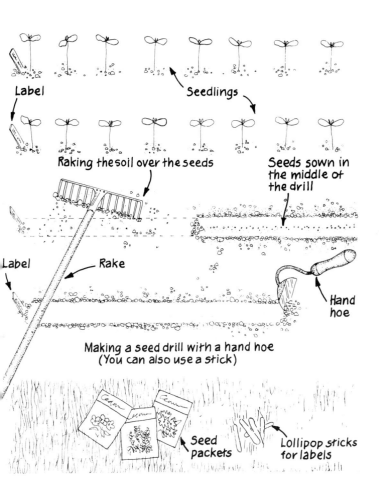

Label

Seedlings

Raking the soil over the seeds

Seeds sown in the middle of the drill

Label

Rake

Hand hoe

Making a seed drill with a hand hoe
(You can also use a stick)

Seed packets

Lollipop sticks for labels

Seedlings

Thin out your seedlings by hand, once or twice, by taking out the smaller, weaker plants. Remove any weeds. Thin out when the seedlings have two or three true leaves. Make the soil firm around the seedlings that you leave. The seed packet will tell you how far apart they should be. You may be able to replant some uprooted seedlings if there are gaps in the rows.

Water the gaps before replanting and always pick up seedlings by the leaves, as their stems are easily hurt.

In dry weather do not forget to water your seedlings. Put a rose (a cap with holes in it) on the end of the watering-can spout. This makes the water come out in a fine spray. A heavy stream of water would knock your seedlings over.

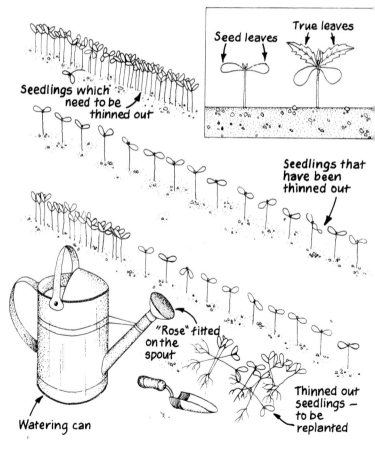

Seedlings which need to be thinned out

Seed leaves

True leaves

Seedlings that have been thinned out

"Rose" fitted on the spout

Watering can

Thinned out seedlings — to be replanted

Keeping your Plants Healthy

Your plants may be attacked by pests or diseases. Try not to treat them with chemical insecticide, as this may kill helpful insects as well as the pests.

Wash the leaves that have pests with warm, slightly soapy water. If your plants are very badly attacked, ask an adult to help you use a chemical.

Peg some strands of black cotton over young plants to prevent birds from eating them.

Water your plants regularly. Do not water in direct sunlight, as this can burn the leaves and the water will dry up too quickly.

Cut dead leaves, branches and dead flowers off your plants. Do not let weeds take over your garden. Weed the flower beds often.

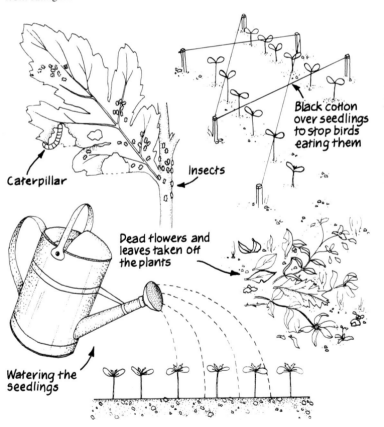

Caterpillar

Insects

Black cotton over seedlings to stop birds eating them

Dead flowers and leaves taken off the plants

Watering the seedlings

Growing Perennial Plants

The plants on these pages are perennials. Perennial plants have soft green stems and leaves. They are not woody like trees and shrubs. They can be tall like the Hollyhock or small like the Primula. Unlike annual plants (see pages 50-51) which only live for a year, perennials live for many years.

In autumn the flowering stems die back to the roots. The plant will store food for the winter in its roots or, like the Iris, in special underground stems (see page 56). Cut down the dead stems to ground level. In spring, they will grow up again and most will flower in the summer.

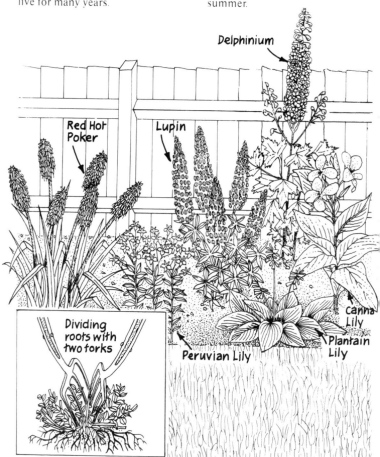

Delphinium

Red Hot Poker

Lupin

Canna Lily

Plantain Lily

Peruvian Lily

Dividing roots with two forks

Plant your perennials in the spring. When perennial plants have been growing for three years they may need to be divided to make stronger, smaller plants. Dig up the roots in the winter. Gently push two forks back-to-back into the middle of the roots and ease them apart. Then replant the younger of the divisions. Be careful – some plants, such as the Paeony, do not like to be divided until they are at least three years old.

The taller perennial plants need support. Tie straight-growing ones, such as Delphiniums and Hollyhocks, to bamboo canes. Push long twigs into the ground in a circle around bushy plants, such as Golden Rod, when the plant is 30-45 centimetres tall.

The Hollyhock may need to be tied to a cane

Hollyhock

alse Goatsbeard

Iris

Oriental Poppy

How to tie a tall plant to a bamboo cane

Primula

Elephant's Ears

Bulbs and Corms

Some flowers are grown from bulbs or corms, not from seeds. A bulb is a bunch of swollen, fleshy leaf-bases, wrapped around one another. A corm is a swollen underground stem, with a thin covering of dry leaves. Both are full of stored food and both are planted underground.

When planted, most will come up year after year. Remove the flowers when they are finished. Plant them with a trowel, as far down in the soil as the bulb or corm is tall, not usually deeper than ten centimetres.

Both will need a lot of water, but be sure the water can drain away completely. Plant them in the autumn if they flower in spring; plant them in early spring if they flower in autumn.

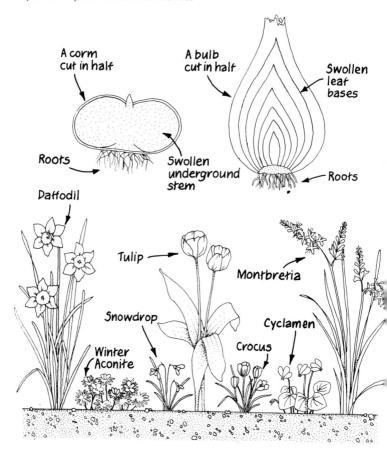

A corm cut in half

A bulb cut in half

Swollen leaf bases

Roots

Swollen underground stem

Roots

Daffodil

Tulip

Montbretia

Snowdrop

Cyclamen

Winter Aconite

Crocus

Window Boxes

If you have not got a garden, you can still grow plants in window boxes. Make your own from wooden boxes, orange crates, or plastic containers. Punch holes in the bottoms and put in stones so that the water can drain off. You can plant bulbs in the autumn to flower the next spring. When the bulbs have finished, store them in a dry place for next year. Change the soil in the boxes and plant annuals such as Alyssum, Petunias and Nasturtiums, for summer flowering. Read up about the flowers – some may need to be planted alone, or may be too tall for boxes.

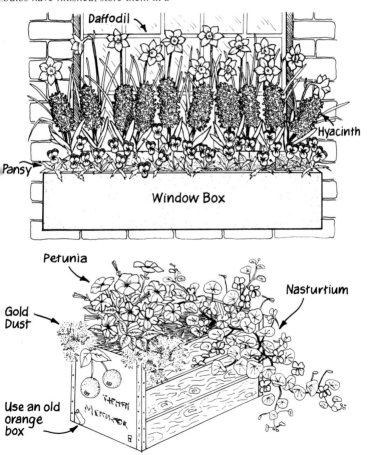

Daffodil

Hyacinth

Pansy

Window Box

Petunia

Nasturtium

Gold Dust

Use an old orange box

Making a Record Book

Keep a record book of the flowers you grow. It can be a useful check-list for next year's garden. If you use a ring-binder, you can always add pages for more flowers. Make coloured drawings of your plants. Note where in the garden you planted the flowers, when you planted them, the months they bloomed, when you thinned out the seedlings, and how tall the plants grew. If the flowers had pests, write down how you treated them. You can watch the insects and birds that are attracted to the flowers, and make notes and drawings of them.

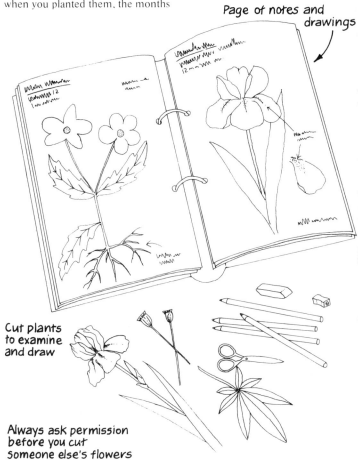

Page of notes and drawings

Cut plants to examine and draw

Always ask permission before you cut someone else's flowers

Books to Read

For looking up the names of garden flowers, the best books to use are *The Dictionary of Garden Plants in Colour* R. Hay & P. M. Synge (Ebury Press & Michael Joseph). This has lots of good colour photographs. *The Observer's Book of Garden Flowers* D. Pycraft (Warne). Cheap and easy to carry. *Ladybird Garden Flowers* B. Vesey-Fitzgerald (Ladybird Books). Both are cheap and worth buying.

If you want to learn a bit more about the parts of flowers and how flowers live, *Piccolo Picture Book of Flowers* G. Surdival (Piccolo Picture Books) has good pictures, is simply written and cheap.

Three good gardening books are: *Gardening: How to Grow Things* Practical Puffin (Penguin), *Gardening* Toppers Activities (Macdonald), and *Mr Smith's Flower Garden* Geoffrey Smith (BBC). They are all fairly cheap, have lots of pictures, and give good hints on making hanging baskets and window boxes.

Clubs to Join

There is probably a local gardening club or horticultural society in your area, which may have a junior section. Get the address from your local library. If you grow flowers, you can show them at your society's flower show. Adult members will also help you with any gardening problems you may have.

There are beautiful parks and gardens in every city and these are open to the public. You will learn a lot about gardening and garden flowers if you visit one of them. Find out if there is one near where you live.

If you get really interested, try setting up your own gardening club with some friends.

Latin Names

Below are the Latin names for all the flowers in this book.

If you want to look up a flower in another book, look up the Latin name in the index.

Blue Flowers

p.6 Ceanothus veitchianus
Delphinium
Muscari armeniacum
p.7 Nigella damascena
Agapanthus campanulatus
Myosotis alpestris
p.8 Gentiana asclepiadea
Campanula carpatica
Echinops ritro
p.9 Vinca minor

Ipomoea tricolor
Chionodoxa luciliae
p.10 Hibiscus syriacus
Scabiosa caucasica
Scilla sibirica
p.11 Lobelia erinus
Centaurea cyanus
Anchusa azurea

Purple Flowers

p.12 Aubrieta deltoidea
Wisteria sinensis
Geranium ibericum
p.13 Syringa vulgaris
Aster novae-belgii
Primula denticulata
p.14 Rosmarinus officinalis
Nepeta mussinii
Hosta fortunei

Latin Names (continued)

Index

Scorecard

The flowers in this scorecard are arranged in the same order as they appear in the book. When you go spotting, fill in the date at the top of one of the blank columns, and then write in that column your score, next to each flower that you see. At the end of the day, add up your scores and put the total at the bottom of the columns. Then add up your grand total.

Page	Species (Name of flower)	Score	Date	Date	Date	Page	Species (Name of flower)	Score			
6	Californian Lilac	15				12	Cranesbill	15			
6	Delphinium	10				13	Lilac	10			
6	Grape Hyacinth	10				13	Michaelmas Daisy	5			
7	Love-in-a-Mist	15				13	Primula	15			
7	African Lily	20				14	Rosemary	10			
7	Forget-me-not	5				14	Catmint	15			
8	Willow Gentian	25				14	Plantain Lily	15			
8	Bellflower	15				15	Hebe	10			
8	Globe Thistle	20				15	Buddleia/ Butterfly Bush	5			
9	Periwinkle	10				15	Lavender	5			
9	Morning Glory	10				16	Magnolia	10			
9	Glory-of-the Snow	10				16	Rose Campion	20			
10	Hibiscus	20				16	Elephant's Ears	20			
10	Scabious	15				17	Weigela	10			
10	Winter Squill	15				17	Pink	10			
11	Lobelia	5				17	Rhododendron	5			
11	Cornflower	10				18	Cyclamen	20			
11	Alkanet	15				18	Hollyhock	10			
12	Aubretia	10				18	Camellia	15			
12	Wisteria	10				19	Begonia	10			
		Total						**Total**			

Page	Species (Name of flower)	Score				Page	Species (Name of flower)	Score			
19	Belladonna Lily	25				27	Day Lily	20			
19	Stonecrop	15				27	Crown Imperial	25			
20	Fuchsia	5				27	Nasturtium	5			
20	Oriental Poppy	15				28	Orange Ball Tree	20			
20	Ornamental Quince	20				28	Globe Flower	15			
21	Escallonia	15				28	Peruvian Lily	20			
21	Oswego Tea	20				29	French Marigold	5			
21	Rosa Moyesii	15				29	Californian Poppy	10			
22	Sweet William	10				29	Geum	10			
22	Red Hot Poker	20				30	White Evergr'n Magnolia	15			
22	Bottle Brush	25				30	Evergreen Candytuft	5			
23	Paeony	10				30	Snowdrop	5			
23	Canna Lily	20				31	Chrysanthemum maximum	10			
23	False Goatsbeard	20				31	Wedding Bells	15			
24	Scarlet Sage	5				31	Pampas Grass	15			
24	Love-lies-bleeding	20				32	Mock Orange	10			
24	Japanese Rose	5				32	Japanese Anemone	15			
25	Fig Marigold	25				32	Lily of the Valley	10			
25	Geranium	5				33	Mexican Orange	20			
25	Flowering Currant	10				33	Baby's Breath	15			
26	Evergreen Azalea	5				33	Christmas Rose	20			
26	Montbretia	15				34	Rock Cress	10			
26	Pot Marigold	10				34	Viburnum tinus	15			
	Total						Total				

Page	Species (Name of flower)	Score				Page	Species (Name of flower)	Score			
34	Madonna Lily	20				42	Polyanthus	5			
35	Daffodil	5				42	Lupin	5			
35	Wallflower	5				42	China Aster	10			
35	Forsythia	5				43	Hyacinth	5			
36	Rock Rose	15				43	Clematis	10			
36	Sunflower	5				43	Zinnia	10			
36	Gold Dust	15				44	Pansy	5			
37	Winter Aconite	20				44	Dahlia	5			
37	Golden Rod	10				44	Crocus	5			
37	Senecio	10				45	Hybrid Tea Rose	5			
38	Rose of Sharon	5				45	Foxglove	5			
38	Evening Primrose	15				45	Phlox	15			
38	Oregon Grape	10				46	Beard Tongue	15			
39	Broom	5				46	Flag Iris	10			
39	Cone Flower	15				46	Tulip	5			
39	Milfoil	10				47	Sweet Pea	5			
40	Potentilla	5				47	Snapdragon	5			
40	Leopard's Bane	10				47	Hydrangea	5			
40	Honeysuckle	5				48	Petunia	5			
41	Winter Jasmine	5				48	Gladiolus	10			
41	Sneezeweed	20				48	Colombine	10			
41	Tickweed	15									
	Total						Total				
							Grand Total				